Nature in the EXTREME

Volcanic ERUPTIONS
by Marian Calabro

San Francisco

by Meish Goldish

GLOBE FEARON

Pearson Learning Group

Contents

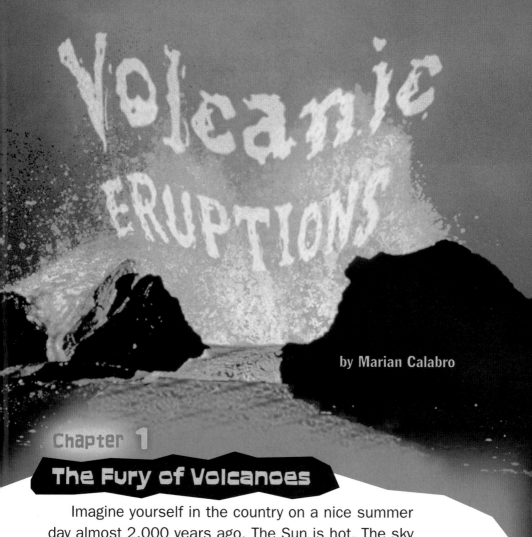

Volcanic Eruptions

by Marian Calabro

Chapter 1

The Fury of Volcanoes

Imagine yourself in the country on a nice summer day almost 2,000 years ago. The Sun is hot. The sky is a bright shade of blue. You are surrounded by fields of grapes and beans.

Suddenly an odd cloud **formation** appears. It seems to rise from a local mountain, Mount Vesuvius. Within seconds, the sky turns a dark gray. Ash and rocks rain down. Foul-smelling fumes make it hard to breathe. You start to run, trying to escape the terror.

This event really happened. On August 24, 79 CE, a terrifying volcanic eruption occurred near the city now known as Naples, Italy. It buried two towns: Pompeii and Herculaneum.

Get ready to read about the dramatic world of volcanoes. You will learn a number of things about these rumbling, lava-belching giant structures. For instance, did you know that volcanoes cluster around a **portion** of the western United States? You'll learn how some volcanoes **enlarge** to form enormous columns of poisonous gases. You'll also read about the death and devastation that volcanoes can cause.

Like a time traveler, you will go back 600,000 years to witness a volcanic eruption. It was so huge that evidence of it can still be seen today. You will then travel forward in time to the eruption of Mount Vesuvius in Italy. You will learn how the people of Pompeii were buried by ash and "frozen" for eternity.

Next, you will be transported to Tambora, Indonesia, in 1815. On that small island, one single volcano spewed out so much **debris** that it blocked the Sun's rays for three days. Winds carried the volcanic particles for thousands of miles. These particles affected the weather worldwide. The amount of sunlight was dimmed, and there was little warmth from the Sun. As a result, people around the globe had "a year without a summer."

Hold your ears! Your next stop will take you to the explosion on Krakatau. A volcano on this island, also in Indonesia, erupted in 1883. The eruption created some of the loudest noises ever heard. People as far as 2,500 miles away heard the explosive booms.

Finally, we will take a look at a volcano that lies simmering in the United States. Mount St. Helens in Washington State violently erupted in 1980. The force of the eruption caused the mountain to lose 1,300 feet of its height! The eruption ended, but Mount St. Helens stayed awake. In 2004, it threatened to explode again.

There's nothing tame about volcanoes. Some volcanoes can erupt with greater force than dynamite. The results can be devastating. Read on and get ready for a wild ride.

The Birth of a Volcano

Volcanoes can blast their fiery contents for miles and miles. Volcanoes can smother anything in their **vicinity** with poisonous gases and ash. Where do volcanoes get their awesome power?

Every volcano starts with an opening in Earth's surface. This opening is called a vent. A vent can be found in the ground or in the ocean floor. Tremendously hot material from within Earth pours out of these openings. After many, many years, the hardened material can form volcanic mountains. Although some erupting volcanoes can form mountains, not all mountains are formed this way. Most mountains aren't volcanoes.

What causes a vent to form? To answer this question, it helps to look at how Earth is constructed. It consists of three layers: the crust, mantle, and core. The crust, made of rock and dirt, is what we stand on. This layer also includes the ocean floor. The crust is about 20 to 30 miles thick. Below the crust is the mantle, a layer of hot liquid rock about 1,800 miles thick. Below the mantle is the core, or the center of Earth. It is about 2,000 miles thick.

The crust feels solid and **secure**, doesn't it? It's actually made of slabs of rock called tectonic plates. One plate can be hundreds of miles across. The plates fit together, like huge pieces of a jigsaw puzzle. These plates move very slowly over the hot liquid rock of the mantle.

Sometimes, two plates can collide. When they do, can you guess what happens? Scorching hot liquid rock can shoot out. When this explosion occurs, a volcano is born!

Chapter 2
When Plates Collide

When two plates collide, one plate usually pushes over the top of the other. The edge of the lower plate is forced down into Earth's mantle. This edge starts to melt because the mantle is much hotter than the crust. The melted material is called magma. Magma can get as hot as 2,000 degrees Fahrenheit. You could melt glass at that temperature!

Magma rises because it isn't as dense and heavy as the crust. It makes its way through the vents created by the collision of the plates. From some volcanoes, magma shoots out like dynamite. From others, magma seeps out in a gentle flow. How do you know how magma will act? The answer depends on how much gas is in the magma. The more gas there is, the more explosive the eruption. Once magma erupts onto Earth's surface, it is called lava.

Volcanoes can also form when two of Earth's plates pull apart. This area is called a rift zone. Most rift zones are found in ocean floors. There's a huge one beneath the Atlantic Ocean. It is located between Europe and North America. Volcanoes erupt there with great **frequency**, but no one sees them.

The magma rising through the rift zone has created a mountain chain under the ocean. The only area above water is Iceland. This country is a North Atlantic island nation. For that country's citizens, **dwelling** among volcanoes is a fact of life.

The 1980 eruption of Mount St. Helens in Washington State hurled rock and ash across the land at speeds of up to 670 miles per hour.

More than half of all land volcanoes form along the Pacific Ocean's "Ring of Fire." This giant circular area touches many countries. Among them are Japan, Indonesia, Mexico, and some nations in South America. Alaska and the American northwest are also within the ring.

Volcanologists are scientists who study volcanoes. These scientists have identified "hot spots" in Earth's mantle. At hot spots, very hot magma has worked its way close to Earth's surface. Areas over these spots are likely to have volcanoes.

The islands of Hawaii lie over a hot spot. The tectonic plate that the islands are located on has slowly been passing over the hot spot for millions of years. Those islands that have already passed over the hot spot no longer have active volcanoes. The islands that are currently above the hot spot have erupting volcanoes.

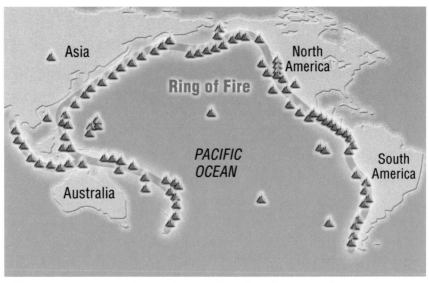

Many volcanoes are located around the Pacific Ocean. Can you guess why this area is called the "Ring of Fire"?

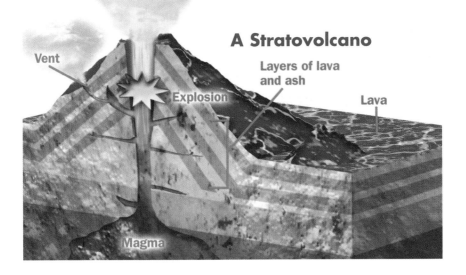

A Stratovolcano

Vent

Layers of lava and ash

Explosion

Lava

Magma

Types of Volcanoes

When you think about a volcano, you probably picture a fiery mountain. It is spewing dark gases and lava. That type of volcano is called a stratovolcano. Stratovolcanoes are steep mountains with layers of hardened lava and ash.

Did you know that some volcanoes don't look like mountains at all? A volcano that erupts with tremendous force can actually lose its peak. The peak doesn't blow off. It collapses into itself. This massive collapse forms a huge pit. The pit is called a crater, or caldera. You'll read about volcanoes whose explosive eruptions created calderas.

Not all volcanoes are violent. A shield volcano is relatively tame. Lava quietly flows from a shield volcano. This type of volcano is **moderately** sloped because the lava hardens in the shape of a shield.

Luckily, the violent types of volcanoes often show signs before they erupt. The ground may shake with small earthquakes, or tremors. Gases escape into the air. If you hear warnings about a volcanic eruption, take **heed**. Eruptions can happen fast. By listening to warnings, **bystanders** can escape injury and even death.

Chapter 3

Ancient Eruptions

Imagine a huge pit in the ground blasted by thousands of sticks of dynamite. Did you ever think a volcano could carve out a huge piece of Earth? One volcano did just that more than 600,000 years ago.

A volcanic eruption created a caldera, or pit, in Earth's surface. The caldera is bigger than the state of Rhode Island! This eruption took place in an area of the United States called Yellowstone National Park.

Most of Yellowstone is in the state of Wyoming. Small **portions** extend into Idaho and Montana. The whole area rests on a hot spot. About 2 million years ago, the first of three volcanic eruptions took place. The eruptions were pretty destructive. In fact, after the first eruption, the American West was covered with more than 3 feet of ash! However, the last eruption, about 600,000 years ago, was so powerful that it made the ground above it collapse. This immense eruption formed the giant caldera that covers much of Yellowstone.

All of the eruptions helped shape the park into a damp, murky, fascinating place. The surface of Yellowstone is like a stove with weird things cooking on top. For example, the park is home to 10,000 bubbling hot springs. Old Faithful is a geyser that shoots hot water high into the air from one of the springs. **Bystanders** get to watch the display about every 45 to 90 minutes.

There are also plenty of vents where steam escapes from Earth. Pools of boiling dirt called mudpots also abound. Sulfuric gases emerge with the water and mud. Can you guess what the gases smell like? They smell like rotten eggs!

These thermal features make Yellowstone an area unlike any other. *Thermal* means "heat-related." The heat that powers the geysers, hot springs, vents, and mudpots comes from the superheated magma that lies under the park.

In fact, Yellowstone is Earth's largest hydrothermal, or hot-water, system. About half of the world's thermal features are found in the main caldera. Some are also found in the smaller calderas that overlap the main caldera. No other area can boast so many geysers. Yellowstone has more than 300.

Thanks to past volcanic activity, Yellowstone also has a special lake. As water collected in a **portion** of the 600,000-year-old caldera, it created Yellowstone Lake. Scientists have made interesting discoveries on the lake's bottom. For one thing, the park's hot spot causes the lake to rise and sink by up to 1 inch each year. The lake also has a crack under it. Scientists don't believe that these features indicate the formation of a new volcano.

Elsewhere in the park, there are plenty of other **formations** for scientists to study. However, no one can directly examine the hot spot under the park. The magma in the hot spot sits 125 miles below ground!

Studies show that Yellowstone is still full of volcanic activity. One study found that the surface of the park has risen 27½ inches in the past 100 years. Slowly, the pressure under the surface pushes up the ground. Earthquakes also occur in and around Yellowstone with **frequency**. Most are so small, though, that they can't be felt.

Some scientists believe that Yellowstone may soon **undergo** another volcanic eruption. Another eruption would not only destroy the park, but could also cause widespread disaster. Widespread disaster would occur because the sources of two major rivers are found in the park. An eruption would fill the Snake and Missouri rivers with ash. The clogging would cause major flooding. The floods, in turn, would damage many farms. The ash from a major eruption would also affect many states.

However, other scientists predict that another eruption will not occur again for centuries. To them, the park is a living laboratory. In addition to thermal features, Yellowstone has a huge variety of animals to study. There are also fossils of animals and plants that lived millions of years ago!

Hot springs can be found throughout Yellowstone National Park. The water temperatures in some springs can get as high as 700 degrees Fahrenheit.

Taken by Surprise

Remember Mount Vesuvius? It was the volcano that erupted in Italy almost 2,000 years ago. Although it wasn't the most powerful ancient eruption, it might be the most famous. A **bystander** took notes. So we have an eyewitness report!

The reporter was Pliny the Younger, a Roman writer. He was staying with his uncle, Pliny the Elder, at the family's country house near Pompeii. When Mount Vesuvius erupted, the younger Pliny was 20 miles away. That distance was close enough to experience the disaster without getting hurt. He told of earthquakes, giant waves in the nearby Bay of Naples, and clouds of volcanic dust.

People in the **vicinity** knew Mount Vesuvius was a volcanic mountain. However, the volcano had not "blown" for hundreds of years. The eruption came as a shock. Pliny wrote that the mountain looked like "a pine tree." The huge column of lava, fire, and rock "rose into the sky on a very long 'trunk' from which spread some 'branches.'"

Pliny the Elder was in charge of a fleet of boats in the bay. He quickly organized rescue teams to evacuate people. Many were saved. Sadly, the elder Pliny died. Ashes from the eruption most likely clogged his lungs.

The nephew relayed his uncle's description of the coast: "...The shoreline moved outwards, and many sea creatures were left on dry sand. Behind us were frightening dark clouds, rent by lightning...opening to reveal huge figures of flame...."

For a full day, the terror did not **decrease**. Imagine being caught in "a darkness that was not like a moonless or cloudy night but more like the black of closed and unlighted rooms. You could hear women lamenting, children crying, men shouting."

Unearthing Pompeii

Although Pliny the Younger survived, many did not. Streams of boiling hot lava and mud flowed downhill from Mount Vesuvius. The air was filled with poisonous gases and fumes. Showers of hot, wet ashes covered Pompeii and Herculaneum. Pompeii was a small, busy town. Herculaneum was a smaller town nearby.

Undoubtedly, some people immediately tried to run for cover. Others may have waited too long to flee. The angry volcano stopped people and animals in their tracks. The daylong eruption was sneaky, too. Pliny reported: "The fire actually stopped some distance away, but darkness and ashes came again, a great weight of them."

Finally, the eruption came to an end. Most of Pompeii lay covered with a sooty blanket. As years went by, the volcano erupted again. It **refreshed** the amount of ash on Pompeii and Herculaneum. Both towns became hidden from sight.

Pompeii remained hidden until the 1700s. The area had become farmland again. One day, a farmer was digging in a field. He hit something hard. Exploring farther, he found the top of a wall from an ancient town.

After years of excavation, Pompeii emerged in amazing detail. The volcanic ash had preserved the town's **dwellings**. Homes displayed stately pillars and grand front doors. Within the homes, bowls of fruits and nuts were found. Scientists found **portions** of eggs placed on a table for a meal! Public sites also remained. Sculptures stood in town squares. There were paved streets, theaters, and even a gymnasium.

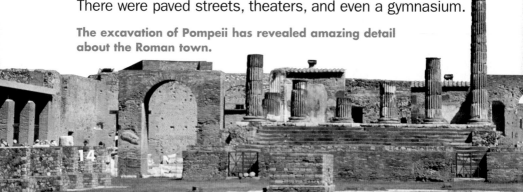

The excavation of Pompeii has revealed amazing detail about the Roman town.

14

Herculaneum has also been excavated. Both ancient towns are popular with tourists. These well-preserved sites are like time capsules from the era of the Roman Empire. From them, we can get a better idea of the culture and way of life back then.

Also discovered were about 2,000 victims caught in the volcano's ash. After the ash cooled and dried, it had hardened around them. As a result, each body was encased in a kind of cast.

In the 1860s, a scientist filled the casts with plaster and then removed the casts. The bodies within the casts had rotted, but the impressions that they made remained. This **technique** created replicas of the people who had died. These statuelike replicas reveal the expressions of terror on the faces of people as they died.

These remains reveal the sheer power of a volcano. Picture the amount of dust and ash it took to bury just one of the towns. In addition, the force of the eruptions must have been so great that people were instantly covered and "frozen" in ash!

Ashes from the eruption hardened around the victims of Mount Vesuvius.

Chapter 4

Tambora: Year Without a Summer

Can you imagine a summer so cold that you have to bundle up to go outside? How would you feel about a summer vacation with snow instead of warm sunshine?

North America and parts of Europe suffered such a summer in 1816. That summer was an entire year after the great volcano Tambora erupted on the other side of the world. No wonder 1816 has gone down in history as "the year without a summer."

Tambora is a volcano in Southeast Asia. This mighty volcano is located on the island of Sumbawa in Indonesia. Sumbawa is found in the Indian Ocean, north of Australia.

Although it was a known volcano, Tambora had been inactive for thousands of years. It had been so quiet that most of the people who lived nearby weren't concerned. Perhaps there were people who did feel uneasy, but what could they do? In the 1800s, there were no easy ways to escape from an island.

Like a sleeping giant, Tambora awakened with a roar. The date was April 10, 1815. The eruption registered a 7 on the Volcano Explosivity Index (VEI). The VEI is a scale that measures the force of a volcano. The scale measures the height of eruptions and how much lava emerges. The index only goes up to 8, so Tambora was a major eruption. In fact, the 1815 eruption of Tambora may be the most powerful eruption of a volcano in recorded history.

The eruption was so fast and so powerful that only a handful of **bystanders** survived. Yet, Tambora did send out some warning signals. Some weeks in advance, the island began to **undergo** tremors.

The tectonic plates under the island were pushing against each other forcefully. Magma began to flow up through rocks. This action caused the ground to shudder, shift, and rumble.

Earthquakes! They made such noise that people who were miles away heard them. The sounds were so loud that they worried a foreign naval officer stationed on another island. He feared that a fierce battle had begun at sea. With other officers, he set out in a ship to investigate. They expected to find cannons and gunfire. They found nothing.

Maybe people were preoccupied with the shaking of the ground. For whatever reason, they ignored the explosive sounds from Tambora. No one **heeded** the volcano's clear warnings.

The Volcanic Explosivity Index (VEI)

VEI	DESCRIPTION	HEIGHT OF CLOUD COLUMN	DURATION OF ERUPTION	EXAMPLE (date of eruption)
0	Nonexplosive	Less than 100 m	varies	Mt. Kilauea, United States (Currently active)
1	Small	100–1,000 m	Less than 1 hour	Nyiragongo, Africa (1982)
2	Moderate	1–5 km	1–6 hours	Galeras, Colombia (1992)
3	Moderate/large	3–15 km	1–12 hours	Ruiz, Colombia (1985)
4	Large	10–25 km	1–12 hours	Kelut, Indonesia (1990)
5	Very large	More than 25 km	6–12 hours	Mount St. Helens, United States (1980)
6	Very large	More than 25 km	More than 12 hours	Krakatau, Indonesia (1883)
7	Very large	More than 25 km	More than 12 hours	Tambora, Indonesia (1815)
8	Very large	More than 25 km	More than 12 hours	Yellowstone caldera, United States (600,000 years ago)

What did the islanders see when Tambora finally erupted? Only one report exists. It was written by Sir Thomas Raffles. Raffles was the British lieutenant governor of Java. Java is an island near Sumbawa. Raffles sought out eyewitnesses.

A Sumbawa islander described the scene. He spoke of "three columns of fire rising to a great height." The man's words have been translated, of course. Yet even in the translation, we can sense the horror of the event. "Soon," he said, "the whole side of the mountain next to the village of Sang'ir seemed like one vast body of liquid fire."

He went on to say: "The glare was terrific, until towards evening, when it became partly obscured by the vast quantities of dust, ashes, stones, and cinders thrown up from the crater....The ashes and stones began to fall...all 'round the neighborhood of the mountain."

Many scientists have studied the eruption of Tambora. They believe its fiery column rose from 24 to 28 miles high. Scientists also speculate that the eruption produced many fast-moving flows of hot air, ash, and lava. These types of flows are the freight trains of volcanic activity. They can easily destroy anything in their path.

Tambora also belched out vast quantities of dark, sooty ash. Darkness then fell around the volcano. It was impossible to see anything. Finally, after five days, the eruption stopped.

On Java, rain fell. It washed away some of the ash and **debris.** The rain helped **refresh** the air and also kept the crops alive. People on the nearby island of Java were able to live through the disaster. The residents of Sumbawa were not as lucky. When the sky cleared, they saw the complete ruin of their island. There were no homes, trees, or crops. Nothing was left.

Snowmen in Summer

Most scientists agree that the 1815 eruption of Tambora caused destruction unmatched in recorded history. Unbearable heat, raging fire, and lava flows rushed into villages. **Dwellings** crumbled like houses of cards. Large amounts of poisonous gases filled the air.

The eruption of Tambora probably killed at least 10,000 people on the island. There are very few volcanic eruptions in recorded history that have directly killed more people. However, the devastation of Tambora's eruption spread far and wide. Tambora set off a chain of events that severely affected the climate for thousands of miles around. It spewed huge amounts of ash, volcanic dust, and **debris** into the air. This material spread slowly through the atmosphere. As it spread, the Sun's rays were blocked.

Colder, darker weather caused food crops to die. This volcanic "blackout" caused temperatures to drop. In the United States, for example, New England actually had snow in the summer of 1816. Children made snowballs. However, farmers lost their crops and their livestock. Some New Englanders headed west, hoping to find more **moderate** weather. Farmers throughout Europe lost crops, too. Many people died from starvation.

When plants and crops died, rodents often snuck indoors looking for food. They brought fleas that carried disease. Many people became weak and sick. An epidemic of typhus broke out in Europe. Typhus is a disease that causes high fever and a rash. Many people in India caught cholera, an acute intestinal infection. Both diseases can be fatal. Antibiotics and other medicines didn't exist then. As a result of starvation and disease, as many as 80,000 people died. Would you ever have guessed that one volcano could cause such widespread devastation?

Photography didn't exist in 1815. So there aren't any photographs of the eruption. Also, there were no telegraphs, telephones, or computers to help pass information from person to person.

Scientists **rely** on more recent information to understand what happened hundreds of years ago in Indonesia. They study the mountain, the soil, and the movement of the ground. All provide clues to the mystery of Tambora.

No one knows the original height of the volcano. Scientists estimate that the mountain may have been 13,000 feet tall. We do know that the eruption caused the collapse of Tambora's peak. This action created a caldera almost 2,300 feet deep. Tambora's height was **decreased** to just over 9,000 feet.

Volcanic ash can float in the air over long distances. Ashes from Tambora were found as far as 800 miles away. Just think, if ashes from a volcano in Chicago traveled that same distance, they would end up in New York!

This photograph taken from the space shuttle shows that the caldera atop Tambora is so large, it can be seen from space.

Today, wedding ceremonies are a part of the thriving culture that can be found on the island of Sumbawa where Mount Tambora is located.

The Legacy of Tambora

The year without a summer finally passed. People in the United States and Europe planted new crops and started over. Indonesia had a bigger, harder task. Its leaders had to rebuild the island of Sumbawa. Houses had to be rebuilt. Streets had to be dug out from the ash. Everything had to be constructed from scratch.

In 1913, a team of Dutch scientists hiked up Tambora. The scientists found that a new crater had opened in the existing caldera. More than 1,000 feet of lava oozed from it. The **formation** of the new crater indicated that the volcano had erupted again. However, this eruption was much less powerful. In fact, the people living on the island hadn't even noticed the eruption.

In 1947, another team of scientists climbed the volcano. The scientists made another discovery—a freshwater lake. Rainwater had collected on the caldera floor, creating the lake. Scientists are quite sure that volcanic activity continued on Tambora. However, this activity did not have the sheer violence that took place in 1815.

Today, Tambora is home to about a million people. Farmers grow rice, corn, and beans. Sumbawans also raise cattle and mine for gold. The volcano isn't as active as it was 200 years ago. Yet, magma under vents on the island still moves. It bubbles up from time to time.

Chapter 5

Krakatau: The Loudest Volcano Ever

Indonesia is a country made up of about 17,000 islands. Indonesia is on the Pacific Ocean's Ring of Fire. Two major tectonic plates lie beneath the region. These plates frequently push against each other. Collisions of the plates send magma up through Earth's crust, forming volcanoes. As a result, Indonesia has more than 100 active volcanoes. About 76 are known to have erupted. Many inactive ones exist, too. Indonesia experiences earthquakes as well.

As you know from the history of Tambora, Sumbawa is one Indonesian island. It was well populated, but many others were not. An island called Krakatau seems not to have had any **dwellers**. Until 1883, it was virtually unknown.

On August 26, 1883, a volcano on Krakatau erupted with tremendous force. Suddenly, the relatively unknown island earned a place in history. The volcano on Krakatau exploded with blasts heard as far as Australia, about 2,500 miles away. It holds the record as the loudest volcanic eruption ever.

Scientists have studied the conditions after the eruption. They know that Krakatau's volcano had been inactive for at least 200 years. As it erupted, it cast the region into darkness. In 2 days, it "blew" 4 times. By the time the eruptions ended, two-thirds of the island had sunk into the sea!

On the Volcano Explosivity Index (VEI), Krakatau registered a 6. That eruption is just one level below Tambora's. On nearby islands, at least 36,000 people were killed by the huge ocean waves that formed as a result of the eruption. Krakatau ranks as one of the deadliest volcanoes in history.

Scientists believe that the volcano erupted with a force equal to hundreds of nuclear bombs! Like other volcanoes with immense power, it triggered the **formation** of a caldera. Unlike many other volcanoes, though, the huge caldera is underwater. In fact, the caldera was formed by the collapse of two-thirds of the island into the sea.

Can you picture a rock so light it floats? Pumice is a type of volcanic rock. Gases trapped inside make the rock float in water like a sponge. During the eruption of Krakatau, thick blocks of pumice were thrown into the waters. Sailors far out at sea during the eruption reported that pumice prevented their boats from sailing. In fact, months after the eruption, waterways hundreds of miles from Krakatau were clogged with pumice.

Enormous, violent ocean waves also formed. Such **enlarged** waves are called tsunamis. The eruption created tsunamis up to 120 feet, the height of a 12-story building! These walls of water slammed onto nearby islands.

The eruption of Krakatau made front page news in London, England, in 1883. The illustrations show the collapse of Krakatau into the Indian Ocean.

Within minutes, whole villages were destroyed. Islands that were miles away were also struck by the enormous waves. **Dwellers** on those islands climbed trees in order to save themselves from drowning.

Berbice, a ship sailing from New York to Indonesia, found itself caught by Krakatau's eruption. Ash and other fiery material were falling all around and onto the ship. The ship's captain kept a log. Here is his description of the event:

"The ash shower is becoming heavier, and is intermixed with fragments of pumice stone. The lightning and thunder became worse and worse; fireballs continually fell on the deck and burst into sparks. We saw flashes of lightning falling quite close to us on the ship; heard fearful rumblings and explosions....

At 2 a.m. on Monday, the twenty-seventh, the ashes, 3 feet thick, were lying on the ship," the captain continued. "I had to...pull my legs out of the ashy layers to prevent them from being buried...The ashes were hot...they burned large holes in our clothing and in the sails...."

The captain of the *Berbice* must have been a master of sailing **technique**. Despite the disaster, he kept his ship **secure**.

Tourists can witness the mild eruptions of Anak Krakatau from a safe distance.

How did Krakatau affect the rest of the world? For one thing, a tsunami reached the Arabian Peninsula 12 hours after the eruption. The Arabian Peninsula is more than 5,000 miles from the island! The glow in the sky from the eruption could be seen in Europe, a whole continent away. Across the Pacific Ocean, small waves hit the west coast of the United States.

After the eruption of 1883, Krakatau was quiet. Then, in 1925, a small volcanic cone broke through the caldera of the volcano. Krakatau had awakened. A new volcano had been born.

The offspring was named Anak Krakatau, which means "child of Krakatau." At age 2, it began acting up. Eruptions occurred with great **frequency**. Krakatau's child was maturing. The new volcano was **enlarging**. Indonesians hoped that there would not be a large eruption.

Thirty-four years after its birth, Anak Krakatau had **undergone** changes. A team of scientists climbed the "new" volcano to study it in detail. They found that the "baby" had widened to about 1 mile in diameter. It was also 545 feet in height. In addition, they also discovered a second, smaller cone in the caldera.

Activity on Anak Krakatau has not **decreased**. The volcano continues to erupt mildly and to grow. The area also experiences earthquake tremors. Scientists **rely** on modern equipment to monitor the situation. They hope to predict any violent eruptions of Anak Krakatau well in advance.

Chapter 6

Mount St. Helens: A Restless Giant

Would you like to wear a breathing mask on your way to school? Well, some students in the Northwest didn't have a choice. In 1980, a known volcano unexpectedly erupted. The volcano is Mount St. Helens. Long after the eruption, harmful materials still filled the air. Students in towns hundreds of miles away had to protect themselves by wearing breathing masks.

Mount St. Helens is located in the Cascade Mountains in Washington State. Native Americans in the **vicinity** have a legend about the fiery volcano. Their name for it, *Louwala-Clough,* means "smoking mountain." They believe the mountain was once a beautiful young woman named Loowit. She had two suitors, the brothers Wyeast and Klickitat. They were the sons of the Great Spirit Sahale. Loowit refused to choose between the young men. They fought over her. Their fighting destroyed villages and burned forests. The destruction angered Sahale, who killed all three young people. Then, Sahale turned each one of them into a mountain.

Because Loowit was so lovely, Sahale turned her into a beautiful mountain. She is now Mount St. Helens. Wyeast, with his head held high, became Mount Hood in Oregon. Losing Loowit caused Klickitat so much grief that he now bends his head in shame. Klickitat's grief is seen in the flattened peak of Mount Adams in Washington.

Mount St. Helens is named for a British diplomat of the 1700s. His title was Baron Saint Helens. Mount St. Helens also has a nickname, "the Fuji of America." Its majestic presence refers to Mount Fuji, a famous volcano in Japan.

The Giant Erupts

In the mid-1800s, Mount St. Helens had some small eruptions. The number of eruptions had **decreased** by 1857. Not until 1980 did the volcano reawaken. However, it did give warnings.

That spring, earthquakes signaled new activity under the volcano. One shook the area quite violently. Tourists went to the mountain to witness the activity. They **heeded** warnings to keep a safe distance. Often, they could see small eruptions of ash and steam rising from the dome.

On May 18, 1980, a scientist named David Johnston was on duty at an observation station. He was 5 miles north of the main crater. Johnston's job involved a **technique** to monitor changes in gas emissions from the volcano. Changes in gas emission sometimes signal a major eruption. Johnston was in contact with the U.S. Geological Survey. On May 18, at about 8:30 a.m., he sent a message. "Vancouver! Vancouver! This is it." Seconds later, the volcano exploded. The clock may have indicated morning, but the sky turned dark as night. Sadly, Johnston was killed. The area he was stationed at was swept away by the eruption.

Upon eruption, the north side of Mount St. Helens caved in. The sudden collapse released enormous pressure on the magma pool under the volcano. Have you ever shaken a soda can, and then opened it? The soda will shoot out fast in a sharp stream. Scientists call this action a direct, or lateral, blast. This kind of blast took place at Mount St. Helens on a huge scale. Lava, ash, and hot gases shot 12 miles into the sky. Flows of lava streamed down at 50 to 80 miles per hour. The eruption lasted 9 hours. It registered a 5 on the VEI.

Mount St. Helens also caused deadly mudflows. Hot rocks and gases from the eruption melted the snow at the top of the mountain. The icy water mixed with tons of loose rocks and dirt. Nothing in the path of the fast-moving mudflows was **secure**. Trees were uprooted, homes were crushed, and cars were buried.

This devastating eruption killed 57 people. The number of animals killed could not be determined. The eruption flattened a 230-square-mile section of forest. However, its fury did not end in the Northwest. The massive tower of ash blew eastward at 60 miles per hour. Ash filtered down across the United States and Canada. Three days later, remnants of the volcano reached the East Coast.

Once awakened, the volcano stayed restless. From 1980 to 1986 alone, scientists counted 17 dome-building episodes and hundreds of small eruptions. These eruptions have piled lava inside the caldera. So the mountain's dome has grown. By the summer of 2004, the dome within the caldera had risen nearly 1,000 feet.

A tower of ash and smoke rose from the top of Mount St. Helens (right). After the eruption, all objects for hundreds of miles around were buried in ash (above).

Steaming Up Again

In September 2004, Mount St. Helens put the Northwest on alert once more. The crater floor rose about 250 feet in 2 weeks! Magma beneath it was pushing upward. Mild earthquake activity also picked up. Was a repeat of the eruption of 1980 in store?

Scientists weren't alarmed. They believed new eruptions would be **moderate**. Still, the federal government issued an alert in early October. Some residents left the area. Tourists went to "volcano-gaze." Fortunately, the signals died down. The government lowered the alert to an advisory. That message means that there is less risk of danger.

Volcanoes like Mount St. Helens remain unsettled. However, in the past 25 years, technology has helped scientists to accurately predict eruptions. For example, scientists no longer have to get close to a volcano to monitor gas emissions. Remote sensors can gather data from a safe distance. Special helicopters fly over the crater to collect information. If this technology had existed in 1980, David Johnston wouldn't have been so close to the volcano.

Scientists also **rely** on Global Positioning System (GPS) equipment. This technology is used in satellites that orbit Earth in outer space. From space, the GPS can measure very slight movements in mountains on Earth's surface.

Scientists also praise the new instruments that measure changes in a volcano's shape. Volcanoes that are about to erupt can form bulges. These bulges are created by the buildup of gases within the volcanoes. Old systems could detect these changes in one dimension only. Newer ones measure changes in three dimensions. This information gives a more accurate picture. Of course, computers have also gotten more powerful. Scientists are able to analyze data better and share the results more easily.

All volcanoes have lessons to teach us. At Mount St. Helens, education is a direct part of the legacy. Since 1982, Mount St. Helens has been a national volcanic monument. In the area where David Johnston died, an observation and education center was built and named in his honor. It is now called the Johnston Ridge Observatory.

Students of all ages visit the mountain to study volcanoes. It is also a tourist attraction. Mount St. Helens may have inspired a worldwide interest in volcanoes. Surely, it has **refreshed** our interest and amazement of them. One woman who lives near the volcano spoke from experience. In 2004 she declared, "All I can say is you better learn to respect it.... Last time, their worst-case scenario didn't even come close to what happened here."

If you ever visit Mount St. Helens, you can stand inside the Johnston Ridge Observatory. You'll enjoy dazzling views of the crater. There is no doubt that you'll also sense the sheer awe of the "smoking mountain."

The 1980 eruption caused the top of Mount St. Helens to cave in. Although the eruption was devastating, plant life began to grow back.

The Value of Volcanoes

Volcanic eruptions are scary and awesome. Luckily, though, you are unlikely to become a victim of a volcano. Only about 600 volcanoes are active worldwide. Of those 600, only 50 to 60 erupt each year. Most eruptions give warnings. So, if you do live near a volcano, you will usually be alerted to impending danger.

Is there a benefit to volcanoes? Scientists believe that they helped to bring life to our planet. Billions of years ago, Earth had no air, water, or life. However, it did have volcanoes. The lava emitted by them helped form Earth's crust. Volcanic gases helped create air. Steam from volcanoes rose into the air and fell as rain. Floods came and oceans formed. Small life-forms emerged from the oceans. Without volcanoes, scientists say, we would have no land to walk on, air to breathe, or water to drink.

By the way, Earth isn't the only planet with volcanoes. Powerful telescopes and information from space probes tell us that Mars has a big one. The moons of Jupiter and Neptune are dotted with them, too. Do you think volcanoes could help create life on those planets?

Volcanic sites become fertile plant-growing areas. The ash mixes with the soil and helps the soil to hold moisture. Ash also adds nutrients that many plants need. Therefore, volcanoes promote healthy and plentiful plantlife.

In Iceland, heat from volcanic activity even keeps people warm. The country has lots of lava beds. Scientists have found ways to channel the warmth of these lava beds into home-heating systems.

Volcanic mountains and islands are awesome, beautiful, and fascinating. If you visit one, you'll find lots to explore. Just be sure to go when the volcano is sleeping!

San Francisco Shaking!

by Meish Goldish

Chapter 1
Disaster!

When you awoke this morning, you probably stepped onto a firm, flat floor. What if the floor of your home started rolling under your feet when you woke up one morning? You might be tossed and turned by the rolling motion. Your furniture might easily **topple** onto you.

That's exactly how people in San Francisco felt when they awoke on April 18, 1906. They felt as if the ground was "wavelike" below them. Early that morning, a powerful earthquake hit the city. It was one of the worst quakes ever reported in the United States. The ground rumbled and shook. The earthquake hurled people around as if they were rag dolls. It was dangerous and terrifying.

The initial shaking lasted less than a minute. Yet, it caused an enormous amount of **turmoil** and damage. Even worse were the many fires that started as a result of the quake. Fires burned in San Francisco for 3 days. Together, the earthquake and fires badly damaged buildings, and about 250,000 people were left homeless. The number of people killed was close to 3,000. Earthquakes in other countries, such as the 2004 South Asia quake that caused a deadly tsunami, have each taken more than 100,000 lives. Yet the San Francisco quake was a terrible one by American standards.

In 1906, San Francisco was the largest city in the West. It grew rapidly after 1848, when gold was discovered nearby. Thousands of people moved to San Francisco. In less than 60 years, the city had grown from just a few thousand people to about 400,000 residents. Most of them lived in wooden houses. They traveled around the city in trolley cars and cable cars that were powered by electricity.

The broken, zipperlike appearance of this brick street in San Francisco was caused by the quake of 1906.

San Francisco had experienced other earthquakes in the past. The damage was so great in the 1906 quake that experts rated it a 9. Earthquakes were rated on a scale of 1 to 10. The rating of 9 was almost the highest possible rating for destruction. A more accurate scale for measuring earthquakes, the Richter scale, was developed in 1935. This scale has no upper limit, but the largest known earthquakes have had measurements as high as 9.5. Scientists have guessed that the 1906 quake would have measured 7.8 on the Richter scale—a high figure.

By any measurement, the 1906 San Francisco earthquake was one of the most **somber** events in American history. The facts are fascinating and unforgettable. This selection will tell the story. Get ready to experience what happened before, during, and after the rumbling and shaking.

The San Francisco earthquake of 1906 destroyed most of the city. The quake set off damaging fires that burned for 3 days.

Chapter 2

the Quake Hits

Did you ever experience an earthquake? People in the Northwest, including San Francisco, other parts of California, Alaska, and Hawaii, have felt quakes many times. That's because those areas have fault lines running through them. A fault line is a long, deep crack in Earth's upper layer, or crust. One famous California fault line is called the San Andreas Fault. It stretches more than 750 miles, from the southern end of the state north into the Pacific Ocean.

Does it surprise you to learn that the earth has a huge crack in it? Actually, fault lines exist on Earth's crust all around the world. The crust is a layer of rock that runs between 5 and 25 miles deep into the ground. The crust is made up of huge sections of rock called tectonic plates. A fault line is space between the plates.

The plates in Earth's crust are always moving. However, the movement is so slow and deep that you don't feel it. As one plate moves, it pushes against the plate next to it. Over a long period of time, pressure can build up along the fault line between the plates. The pressure can grow to a point where the plates cannot **withstand** it. When the pressure builds to that point, certain areas along the two plates can break apart. This action causes sudden movements in Earth's crust called earthquakes.

Before 1906, energy between rock plates had been building along part of the San Andreas Fault in California. On the morning of April 18, the plates snapped and a tremendous rumbling shook the ground.

The rumbling and shaking didn't stop newspaper workers on this evening edition. Based in the San Francisco Bay area, this paper still went to press on the day of the quake.

The First Shock

In the early morning hours of April 18, 1906, San Francisco was quiet and peaceful. Everything seemed normal that Wednesday morning. No one in the city had any idea that a major earthquake was about to strike. However, if animals could talk, they would have warned of the disaster that was coming. Some animals can sense an earthquake hours or even days before it hits. They can feel very slight trembling in the earth that humans don't notice.

The night before the quake, many horses in San Francisco moved restlessly in their stalls. They snorted loudly and stomped their hooves. On farms outside the city, cows also acted in unusual ways. Farmers were puzzled by their odd behavior.

In the city, many dogs acted strangely. They barked and cried all night long without **tiring**. One dog owner said that her dog raced around the house just before the earthquake struck. It leaped out the window and into the street. Her dog sensed that danger was about to hit.

At 5:12 a.m., the earthquake struck with great force. The first people to experience it were sailors on the Pacific Ocean, about 150 miles off the coast of California. The front of their ship, the *John A. Campbell*, was suddenly **elevated**. It rose up into the air and came crashing down into the water. Shortly afterward, another ship closer to land fell over into the ocean. It was as if a powerful wind had just blown it over.

The United States

California
San Francisco
Los Angeles
Pacific Ocean

The earthquake of 1906 struck along 290 miles of the famous San Andreas Fault.

The earthquake had begun in the ocean. That's because the San Andreas Fault extends into the Pacific Ocean. The shock waves raced along the underwater fault line at 7,000 miles per hour. They were headed toward the California coast. The earthquake struck land about 90 miles north of San Francisco. A lighthouse rocked and then exploded. In the forests along the coast, tall trees **toppled** to the ground. Freight trains overturned as the earth cracked open under the rails.

The earthquake quickly reached San Francisco. Because the time was 5:12 a.m., most people were sleeping when it hit. They were thrown out of bed and tossed across their rooms. Everything went flying. **Amid** the chaos and confusion, people thought the world was coming to an end.

One survivor, Emma Burke, gave her **version** of the quake. She described the earthquake's noise as "deafening." She recalled "the crash of dishes, falling pictures, the rattle of the flat tin roof, bookcases being overturned, the piano hurled across the parlor, the groaning and straining of the building itself, broken glass and falling plaster."

Roofs, chimneys, ceilings, walls, and floors collapsed. People were trapped under tons of brick and wood. Many people were killed instantly.

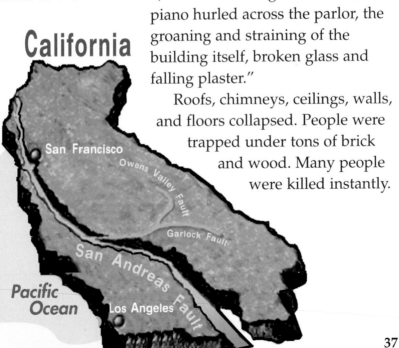

No Escape

Many of the people still alive after the earthquake struck rushed from their homes and into the streets. Some people were alive, but trapped by debris and unable to run into the streets. Most were too terrified to get dressed. They raced outside in their pajamas, nightgowns, and robes. Some didn't even bother to put on shoes.

Yet, the outdoors offered no escape from their **plight**. Many streets had wide, deep cracks in them. As the earth continued to shake, buildings fell onto people. Power lines snapped, breaking electrical **circuits** to homes and businesses. Bricks and wreckage lay everywhere.

One survivor, P. Barrett, later wrote: "All of a sudden we had found ourselves staggering and reeling. It was as if the earth was slipping gently from under our feet. Then came the sickening sway of the earth that threw us flat upon our faces. We struggled in the street. We could not get to our feet.... Big buildings crumbled as one might crush a biscuit in one's hand."

Animals, like people, tried to find safety outdoors. Sadly, many did not succeed. A large herd of cattle was killed when a building collapsed onto it. Other animals died when they fell into the deep cracks in the street.

Few objects could **withstand** the earthquake's power. Trolley cars and cable cars lay on their sides. Their tracks were ripped from the ground and twisted like pretzels. Water shot up from streets in tall fountains. The earthquake had torn apart underground water pipes.

Finally, the rumbling stopped. People hoped that the earthquake was now over. However, 3 hours later, another powerful shock, called an "aftershock," occurred.

No one had been prepared for the quake or its aftershock —and no one was prepared for the fires that followed.

Chapter 3

City on Fire!

Immediately after the earthquake stopped, fires broke out all around San Francisco. The violent shaking of the ground had damaged gas lines and electrical **circuits** around the city. Now, wherever leaking gas met an electric spark, the gas exploded into flames. More fires began when lit gas lamps in homes and offices fell over.

Many of San Francisco's houses and other buildings were made of wood. The wood was a powerful fuel **amid** the hungry flames. Fires traveled rapidly from one neighborhood to another. Within a few hours, many homes across the city were burning. So were hotels, theaters, banks, offices, and other large buildings. In the end, the fires had spread across 490 city blocks.

Some people made the crisis worse. They accidentally started fires of their own. One famous example was the "Ham and Eggs Fire." It began in the western section of San Francisco. A woman thought her house had survived the earthquake. She began to cook breakfast, but she didn't realize that her chimney had collapsed. When she lit her stove, it exploded and a fire began. The wind spread the flames to other homes in the neighborhood. Soon the fire became a major blaze.

A resident named Thomas Jefferson Chase was on his way to work when the fires began. He said, "The street was like looking in the door of a furnace. Flames and smoke rolled with the draft created by the intense heat, rolling up the street with a roar, then up into the air for hundreds of feet. It was an awful sight."

Doomed Buildings

Some of San Francisco's most important buildings were lost even before the fires began. For example, City Hall was a new, $6 million structure. It was the largest building in California. The earthquake sent its walls crashing to the ground. All that was left standing were its steel pillars and dome.

Other buildings survived the earthquake but not the fires. San Francisco's tallest structure was the Call Building. The 22-story building was just 9 years old. Engineers had proudly claimed it was earthquake-proof. Indeed, it successfully **withstood** the violent shaking of the ground on April 18. Only a few decorations on the outside of the building had fallen off.

However, the fires caused by the quake proved to be a much greater challenge. Flames on Third Street headed toward the Winchester Hotel. The Call Building was right next to the hotel. Just before 11:00 a.m., the Winchester caught fire. The heat from the fire was tremendous. It exploded a window on the second floor of the Call Building. The fire crept inside and burned an office. Flames continued into the hallway and made their way into the elevator shaft. The flames then shot up the shaft. Fire reached the top of the Call Building, 312 feet from the ground.

The Call Building was doomed. On each floor, heat from the flames exploded all of the windows. The fire drew fresh air into the building through the broken windows, and the newly fed flames burned the building completely. The fire then jumped to other buildings on the street. By the middle of the afternoon, the Palace Hotel and other large downtown buildings were on fire. Smoke from the rising flames could be seen 100 miles away.

People watched as building after building burned. They could not believe what they were seeing. One survivor of the quake, Peter Bacigalupi, was one of those who watched. As he gazed at the fires, he saw a man crying loudly in the street. Bacigalupi **inquired** about the man's grief.

The stranger pointed to a building. He said, "Don't you see the fire right next to my store? I have $10,000 that I will lose if my store is burned."

Bacigalupi felt sorry for the man. Yet, being a store owner himself, Bacigalupi also saw a quick business opportunity. Bacigalupi knew the grief-stricken owner's building was in a good part of the city. If Bacigalupi bought the store from the owner and if by chance the building didn't burn too badly, Bacigalupi would own a new store in an excellent location.

Bacigalupi offered to rent the building from the **fatigued** store owner for $500. The owner thought about it for several minutes. However, the man refused the deal. Bacigalupi recalled, "While we stood there 15 minutes later, his place was burning fiercely."

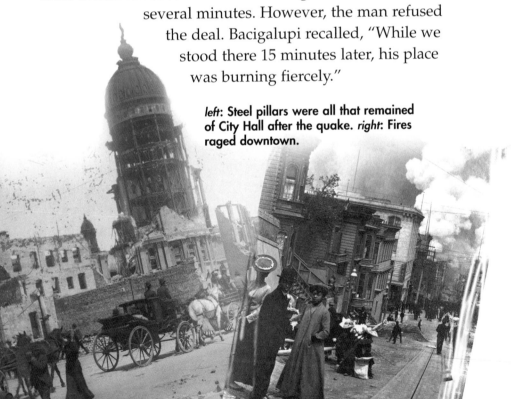

left: Steel pillars were all that remained of City Hall after the quake. *right*: Fires raged downtown.

Fighting the Flames

When the fires broke out, no alarm bells rang. Why? The city's alarm system did not have very advanced **circuitry**. The alarm system ran on simple batteries that sat in glass jars on shelves. When the glass was broken, the alarm would be "tripped," or would go off. The glass jars fell and broke during the earthquake, which made the alarm system useless. The batteries couldn't set off an alarm.

Firefighters didn't need any alarms anyway. They could easily see the fires. What they did need, however, were orders from their boss. They needed to know how to attack the blazing fires. Unfortunately, San Francisco fire chief Dennis Sullivan was unable to give those orders. When the quake struck, he was badly injured by a falling chimney. Fire Chief Sullivan died several days later.

Without their chief, firefighters were unable to get organized quickly. They needed to **inquire** about assignments and instructions. No one seemed to have advice in the middle of all the **turmoil** and confusion. The fires spread out of control throughout the city.

Finally, an army officer, Brigadier General Frederick Funston, took action. He ordered the troops at his army post to battle the flames. Brigadier General Funston then called for more federal soldiers. He told San Francisco's mayor, Eugene Schmitz, that the city was now under military rule. Mayor Schmitz did what he could to better the **plight** of the city's people. He organized more than 1,000 city firefighters and police officers to work with the army troops.

During the 1906 earthquake, the fire department raced to put out fires, even though the water supply was limited.

Unfortunately, battling the blazes was difficult. Very little water ran from any of the city's fire hydrants because water pipes had been torn apart by the earthquake. About 80 million gallons of badly needed water were now escaping into the ground. San Francisco did have a secret supply of water in 24 huge tanks. Each tank held between 16,000 and 100,000 gallons of water. However, only Fire Chief Sullivan knew where the tanks were hidden. He had developed an emergency plan for fighting a major city fire such as this one. His plan included information about the location of the water tanks. Sullivan was now dying from his injuries, so the tanks remained hidden.

Firefighters turned to nearby pools and sewers, as well as San Francisco Bay, for water. They only managed to get a small amount. It was not enough to put out the flames throughout the city. Even if a bucket of water or a working hose was available, it couldn't always be used. The heat of the fire was so great that firefighters often couldn't move close enough to battle the blazes. The water from their hoses turned to steam. As a result, the fires continued to burn.

Without water, firefighters had to find another way to stop the flames from spreading. By afternoon, they received orders to create a firebreak—a large path with nothing in it to burn. Once a fire reaches a firebreak, it has no fuel. It may slow down or stop spreading.

Building the firebreak in San Francisco was an enormous and **tiring** task. The path was to be 1 mile long and nearly 500 feet wide. Firefighters used dynamite and cannons to blow up all structures that stood along the path of the firebreak. They brought down many houses and other buildings that were within the area. The work went on for a 3-day **interval**. Noise from the explosions was deafening.

Saving the Money!

Hundreds of structures fell from fire or exploding dynamite. One important building managed to survive. It was the U.S. Mint, which held $20 million in coins and gold bars. Firefighters, soldiers, and 50 people who worked at the Mint helped save it.

Just 10 days before the earthquake, a new water system had been completed at the Mint. The water came from a well. As a huge fire moved toward the Mint, workers took quick action. They used well water to soak each floor of the building so it would not catch fire. At one point, clouds of smoke poured into the Mint. The workers were unable to breathe. They quickly moved to the building's lowest floor. Once the smoke thinned, they returned to finish the job. They soaked the roof and put out fires that were burning there.

By 4:00 p.m., the Mint was out of danger. The outside of the building had some burn marks, and some pieces of glass were missing. However, the Mint and the money inside it were safe.

Chapter 4

Amazing Escapes and Rescues

Imagine being in a place with buildings **toppling** and fires raging around you. What would you do? About 70,000 residents of San Francisco rushed to escape the city and its **turmoil**. They headed toward San Francisco Bay and the Ferry Building. They hoped to ride a ferryboat from San Francisco across the water to the town of Oakland or to Alameda Island. Both of these places are on the eastern side of the Bay, well away from the fires.

People walked for miles to get to the Ferry Building. Along the way, they heard false rumors that all the ferries had shut down. Some people gave up at that point, but others kept going. Crowds of **fatigued** walkers finally reached the docks. They carried their suitcases and bundles with them. One ticket agent said, "The people all seemed to be in a daze or stunned."

Ticket agents worked as quickly as possible to handle all the passengers. People fought desperately to get onto a ferryboat.

One person, G. A. Raymond, offered this **version** of the events: "There must have been 10,000 people trying to get on that boat. Men and women fought like wildcats to push their way aboard. Clothes were torn from the backs of men, women, and children....Women fainted, and there was no water at hand with which to revive them."

Other people sat or stood patiently in the waiting room of the Ferry Building. An eyewitness named Bailey Millard recalled: "We were 2 hours waiting for gasoline for the launch, and all the time cinders fell upon us and the smoke poured over us, while the red glare of the burning houses was reflected far out upon the dirty, ash-strewn water of the bay."

Not everyone escaped from San Francisco by boat. Most residents remained in the city. They tried to reach safety by moving to **elevated** ground, including the hilly areas of Golden Gate Park. A military base called the Presidio was another place where residents gathered.

Before moving, people collected any personal belongings they could find. They took whatever they could carry, including jewelry, clothing, and kitchenware. Some people even pushed pianos along the rubble-filled streets. Many families brought their pets. One woman had a parrot perched on her hand. She also carried four kittens in a birdcage.

A witness, DeWitt Baldwin, gave this **version** of events: "Folks were carrying bundles, boxes, trunks.... I saw mothers carrying their babies and little children hanging onto their parents' hands. Once in a while a boy's play wagon, on which were clothes and food supplies which would help temporarily, would pass by. These lines of people overflowed the sidewalks and were going toward the mountains beyond the Mission area of the city."

Earthquake victims traveled with their belongings any way they could.

Decision: Move or Stay?

Imagine having to move your belongings without a car or moving van. The residents of San Francisco faced that **somber** challenge after the earthquake struck. Few people owned automobiles, and the army quickly took over any automobiles that were available.

Amid their desperate situation, residents were forced to find creative ways to move their belongings. They used anything with wheels. They piled their belongings onto bicycles, baby strollers, and wheelbarrows. Some families even used roller skates as wheels. People without wheels walked, carrying trunks or suitcases balanced on their heads. Some people had poles across their shoulders with their bags attached. Others carried filled pillowcases, sheets, and blankets over their shoulders. Still others dragged chairs loaded with belongings.

The luckiest people were those who were able to hire a horse-drawn wagon to transport their belongings. Howard T. Livingston recalled that a friend had hired a horse and wagon to move his parents and their possessions. The friend's elderly mother refused to leave her home. The horse and empty wagon stood outside the house for several hours. As the hours passed, the bill for renting the vehicle increased. Finally, as evening approached, so did a distant fire. At that point, two police officers simply picked up the woman and placed her in the wagon!

Is it surprising that some residents refused to leave their homes after the quake? They stayed because they feared being robbed. Thieves risked entering damaged buildings, and looters broke into houses and stores to grab valuables. Some criminals even dared to rob dead bodies in the streets.

Mayor Schmitz took a strict stand against the looters. He ordered police and **federal** troops to shoot anyone caught stealing. Indeed, several looters met their deaths that way. In some cases, ordinary citizens who saw looters became angry and killed them.

Some people who feared being robbed tried to protect their belongings in another way. If they couldn't take items with them, they buried them in the ground. They hoped their belongings would be safe not just from looters, but from the fires as well. However, their plans didn't always succeed.

A doctor named George Blumer described one such incident: "One classmate of mine…had an unfortunate experience. He had many valuable books at his house and also costly Oriental rugs. He dug a hole in his yard in which he deposited the books, surrounded and protected by the rugs. A day or two later, a wrecking crew blew up his house, which collapsed in flames on top of his treasures."

This community pulled together by creating an outdoor kitchen.

Life and Death

The earthquake left thousands of people in a terrible **plight**. Victims were injured or trapped **amid** all the rubble and debris. Some residents were trapped inside their homes. When the earth shifted, so did the houses. This shifting caused doors to jam shut. Other people lay helpless under piles of bricks in the street. Police, firefighters, and army troops worked desperately to rescue as many victims as possible.

David Frazier had been sleeping on a folding bed when the earthquake struck. The shaking caused his bed to fold up—with him in it! Frazier was unable to move or even to breathe easily. A police officer came to his rescue and pulled him to safety.

Sometimes ordinary citizens were the ones who came to the rescue. Many injured people were at Presidio Hospital when its roof caught fire. All the patients had to be removed immediately. Doctors called in volunteers from the street. Any cars that were nearby were put into service.

Six people were needed to move each patient. A doctor recalled, "Three men would get on each side of a patient, two at each end and two at the middle, push their arms under the mattress, clasp hands, and carry out the patient, who was deposited in an automobile." All the patients were moved safely during the **interval** of time before the fire spread to other parts of the hospital.

However, not everyone was rescued in time in other places in the city. As the fires approached, some of these people trapped under bricks and rubble begged soldiers to shoot them. They did not want to be killed by the raging fires. The soldiers **somberly** fulfilled the victims' last wishes.

Rescuers attempted to save animals as well as people. In one case, the earthquake caused the roof of a horse stable to collapse. About 200 horses were trapped in their stalls by the caved-in roof. Also, the stable was very close to San Francisco Bay. Water from the bay rushed through cracks in the ground and floors of the stable. The water level in the stable became so **elevated** that it endangered the horses.

Heroic citizens raced to the rescue. Some people went into the stalls and helped the horses keep their heads above water. Others broke through the stable walls. They created an escape hole for the animals. In the end, all but two of the horses were rescued.

In another case, Charles Kendrick recalled how he and two other men rescued the animals at Robinson's Pet Shop. He said, "We broke in the door and turned loose these creatures, among which were several small monkeys." Kendrick hoped that the animals could survive the city's fires and **turmoil**.

Some horses were victims of falling bricks that struck and killed them during the earthquake. The ones in this picture were lucky to survive.

Coming to the Rescue

Rescuers didn't just save people and animals. They saved property as well. For instance, Alice Eastwood was the head of a museum that housed rare plants and flowers. When fire threatened to burn the building, she worked without **tiring** to save the valuable plants on each floor. Eastwood chose to save the plants rather than her own home. She figured her own belongings would be easier to replace.

Bank owners worked to save their banks' money. One owner, Charles Crocker, told helpers to place the money in large bags. Crocker then, one by one, put the bags on wagons and drove them to the harbor. He paid a boat owner to take the bags to the middle of San Francisco Bay. The boat stayed there until it could safely return to shore with the money.

Unfortunately, not all property rescues succeeded. About a half-dozen men tried to save the artwork in the Mark Hopkins Art Institute. They planned to transfer the art across the street to the Fairmont Hotel. The hotel had been advertised as the first fireproof building in the West.

First, the men broke open the door of the art institute. Then, they spent hours carrying paintings, statues, and other precious objects across the street. They had to force open the hotel doors in order to put the treasures in the hotel lobby. However, their efforts were in vain. When the fire reached the hotel, the building burned badly. The heat was so great that even the granite stone outside the building melted. The art in the hotel lobby was ruined.

If you lived in San Francisco on the day of the 1906 earthquake, you would have seen much of your beloved city on fire. Smoke would have been everywhere. Your home would have been badly damaged. You wouldn't have been able to move back in until the house was **restored**. Your house must have also met safety **codes**. You would have had few possessions and no food or water. What would you have done? You couldn't have done much except try to find a safe place to wait for help to arrive.

City leaders did what they could to help the 250,000 San Franciscans suffering from shock and **fatigue**. For example, about 10 hours after the earthquake hit, Mayor Schmitz appointed a relief committee. The committee set up refugee camps in city parks where homeless residents could sleep. People made tents with items such as blankets, sheets, rugs, and tablecloths.

Some earthquake victims had lost all their belongings, including clothes. The committee set up relief stations around the city for residents who needed clothing. People in this **plight** waited in line to receive shoes, pants, coats, and other necessities.

Other relief stations were organized to provide food. After the earthquake, no stores were allowed to sell food. Instead, people received free food at relief stations. Some lines were five blocks long. Most people stood patiently to get bread, milk, vegetables, and meat.

People also waited for water. The earthquake had broken the city's three main water pipes. No drinking water would be available until the pipes could be **restored**. In the meantime, boats brought water from other towns to the city. People lined up for one bucketful at a time.

Relief stations served entire meals to people who wanted them. At the relief stations, residents ate in large groups for breakfast, lunch, and dinner.

Some houses survived the quake. Homeowners **inquired** anxiously if they might be allowed to cook at home. City officials wouldn't allow them to cook indoors. Stoves in most homes were connected to chimneys. Officials feared there could be a gas explosion if a chimney had been damaged. Residents cooked outdoors instead. They built stoves or made campfires in the street or their yard.

People weren't allowed to light a match or candle inside their homes, either. DeWitt Baldwin recalled how his mother struck a match indoors to light her gas stove. She wanted to heat some milk for her six-month-old baby. Soon a police officer came to the door. He warned her, "Madam, put out that light, and if you do that again I will have to shoot you." The officer was serious. Baldwin's mother obeyed the new safety **code**.

Cooking indoors was prohibited, so these women had to make themselves comfortable while cooking outdoors.

The Days After the Quake

City officials did their best to handle many emergencies after the earthquake. Most of the city's hospitals were destroyed or closed because of damage. On the day of the quake, more than 30 babies were born in Golden Gate Park. Babies continued to be delivered outdoors in the days to come. The city also had to deal with deaths from the quake. Police officers and **federal** soldiers collected hundreds of bodies and drove them to the city morgues.

Another crisis developed when thousands of rats ran loose in the city. The fires had driven the rats out of buildings and into the streets. Health officials feared a deadly disease known as plague might break out because fleas on rats can carry dangerous germs. Officials offered money for dead rats that were brought to them. People used their pets to help them hunt and kill the rats.

Meanwhile, firefighters continued the **tiring** work of dynamiting buildings. They were trying to create a gap to stop or slow the flames from spreading. The constant sounds of explosions could be heard throughout the city.

For 3 days following the quake, there were many unusual sights in San Francisco. Not only did citizens eat and sleep outdoors during this **interval**, but they also tried to relax there. Music provided some relief in the noise and smoke. Some residents moved their pianos outside and played. Crowds gathered around to sing. In spite of the **somber** situation, people tried to keep a sense of humor. Some amusing signs on refugee tents read "The New Palace Hotel," "Ring the Bell for Landlady," or "Rooms for Rent."

Citizens of San Francisco did their best to help one another during their **plight**. One recalled, "There was much kindliness....The strong helped the weak with their burdens."

San Francisco burned for three full days after the earthquake of 1906. The break that firefighters had made failed to stop the flames from spreading. By Saturday, April 21, much of the city was destroyed. On that day, the fires finally went out for two reasons: first, the wind shifted direction. For 3 days the wind had blown from the bay toward the land. On Saturday, it began to blow toward the bay, away from the city. Second, there was almost nothing left to burn. Three-quarters of the city—490 blocks—lay in ashes.

You might expect **fatigued** San Franciscans to give up and declare themselves ruined. Yet, that did not happen. Even though many had lost almost all their belongings, the citizens never lost their spirit. They were determined to **restore** their city. San Franciscan Howard Livingston recalled, "I frequently heard people say that the new San Francisco would be a far finer city than the one which had been destroyed."

Another resident, Peter Bacigalupi, wrote: "I am 51 years old now, and it seems hard for me to start business anew, just as I did 35 years ago, but I am game [willing], and intend to go to it now as I did then…Regardless of all these ordeals, I am going to stick with 'Frisco.'" Frisco was a popular nickname for the city.

The **restoration** of the city became official just 5 days after the quake. George Pardee, the governor of California, stated, "The work of rebuilding San Francisco has commenced, and I expect to see the great metropolis [city] replaced on a much grander scale than ever before."

San Francisco Lives Again!

Some changes in the city came quickly. Mail delivery began again just 2 days after the earthquake. Workers picked up and delivered mail at the refugee camps. Many people had no paper or envelopes. They were allowed to write letters on just about anything, including cardboard and wrapping paper. The post office didn't even require stamps!

Within 2 weeks, water was available around the city. Many electric power lines went back up during this **interval**. People had telephone service once again. Streets were cleared of rubble. Rail tracks were **restored** so that trolley and cable cars could run again. Some grocery stores and restaurants reopened.

As news of the earthquake spread, people across the United States offered help. They sent food, clothing, and bedding to San Francisco. Doctors and nurses traveled to the city to care for people who had been injured. Schoolchildren raised money for a new school. One Oregon school for Native Americans baked 830 loaves of bread for hungry city residents.

Help also came from **federal**, state, and city governments. For example, President Theodore Roosevelt ordered the army to send tents and blankets to San Francisco's refugee camps. That service provided people with a better **version** of a home than their homemade tents had. Residents remained in the camps until their real homes were repaired. They couldn't move back until officials said the gas lines and electrical circuits were safe. In some cases, those repairs took many months.

People stayed in refugee camps throughout the summer. When autumn came, it was too cold for them to sleep in tents. The city built small homes, called refugee shacks, in city parks. When the parks became overcrowded with shacks, the city made a special offer. People could keep their shack for free if they moved it elsewhere. A year after the earthquake, many people began to move out of the refugee camps. They placed their shack on wheels and moved it. A horse or mule pulled it to its new location. The shacks became permanent homes.

After the earthquake, the city also helped to build homes for sick and elderly people. One of these homes was opened in a building that had been a horse stable. Workers had cleaned the floors and made bedrooms, bathrooms, and kitchens for needy residents.

The city also gave money to people to help them reopen their businesses. The number of new businesses and new buildings grew very fast. In just 3 months, the city had about 300 new buildings. Within 6 years, it had 20,000 new buildings.

San Francisco was **restored** quickly. In 1915, just 9 years after the earthquake and fires, it was the host city of a World's Fair. Visitors saw a restored city. They could barely tell that a disaster had ever struck there.

Many people left homeless by the earthquake found shelter in refugee shacks like the ones shown.

A Bright Future

The San Francisco earthquake and fire of 1906 was indeed a terrible tragedy. More than 28,000 buildings **toppled** or burned. More than half the city's population became homeless. Losses totaled more than $400 million. Today, that would amount to billions of dollars.

Yet, the people of San Francisco rebuilt their city. Just days after the 1906 earthquake, Governor Pardee of California made a prediction. He said that San Francisco would recover. He said it would become an even greater city than it ever was before.

Pardee's prediction was certainly correct. San Francisco, the "City by the Bay," grew strong once again. Today, it is one of the largest cities in California. Its population is now nearly double what it was in 1906. Modern San Francisco is an important business center. It is the home of many high-tech companies, banks, universities, and publishing companies. More than 100 major corporations have their headquarters, or main offices, in the San Francisco area.

The city is also popular with travelers and tourists. If you visit modern San Francisco, you can ride cable cars and trolley cars, just like the ones that people rode back in 1906. The city has steep hills and a foggy climate. It also has many beautiful and interesting sights. These sights include Chinatown, Golden Gate Park, and the San Francisco Bay.

Modern San Francisco is truly a remarkable place. Yet because of its size and importance, some people are concerned about its future. People worry about another earthquake. If a quake struck the city today with the same power as in 1906, the results could be disastrous. The loss of life and property could be far greater than it was a century ago.

San Francisco and the rest of California remain at risk for earthquakes. Small quakes occur regularly along the San Andreas Fault. Some of those quakes have been powerful. In 1989, another quake that registered 7.1 struck San Francisco. It was less disastrous than the quake of 1906. Yet, it was still very destructive. More than 100,000 homes were damaged, and dozens of buildings collapsed. Property loss totaled $3 billion. Worst of all, 62 people lost their lives.

Seismologists think an even stronger quake will hit California in the future. They call it "the Big One." The U.S. Geological Survey (USGS) is a **federal** agency that studies earthquakes. What causes people at the agency to worry about "the Big One"? The scientists look at how often large earthquakes have occurred in an area. Then, they assign percentages to the chance of a large quake occurring in the future.

Judging from earthquake activity in the San Francisco region, scientists say that there is about a 62 percent chance that an earthquake measuring 6.7 or higher on the Richter scale will occur in San Francisco before 2032. The chance of an even greater earthquake hitting very soon is much lower. Studies have found that over the past 1,500 years or so, large earthquakes have taken place at about 150-year **intervals** on the southern part of the San Andreas Fault. Considering that the last great earthquake in the San Francisco area was in 1906, that would mean "the Big One" would not be likely to hit until about 2066.

Of course, guesses based on averages can't accurately predict the next major earthquake. Therefore, the USGS watches the movement of land around the fault closely. USGS workers look for changes in **elevation** and other signs that pressure is building in Earth's tectonic plates.

Recall what happened in the San Francisco earthquake of 1906. What has changed since then?

In 1906, buildings and other structures collapsed. Today, USGS findings help government officials decide where to build new schools, hospitals, and power plants. The findings help engineers build bridges and skyscrapers to **withstand** the earth's shaking. Also, structures are now built according to strict safety **codes**. Structures are designed to safeguard the lives of people within and around the structure.

In 1906, fires raged through the city. Today, firefighters and other emergency workers have better training. They know what to do if an earthquake strikes.

In 1906, people did not know what to do to keep safe. Today, people have much better information. In 1990, for example, newspapers in and around San Francisco sent a USGS magazine to 2.5 million homes. The magazine articles told families how to strengthen their houses. It told them how to remain safe during an earthquake.

People who live in San Francisco and all of California can't prevent earthquakes. However, thanks to safety measures, they can hope that their beautiful city will never again be destroyed the way it was in 1906.

Today, many beautiful structures can be found in San Francisco. These structures have earthquake-proof features.

Glossary

amid in the middle of; among

bystanders people who are located near an event but are not caught up in it

circuits paths over which electric currents flow. **Circuitry** is a complete system of electric current.

codes rules or laws

debris scattered pieces of something that has been destroyed or broken down; rubbish or litter

decrease to lessen or make smaller; to cause something to get smaller

dwelling living in a certain place. A **dwelling** is also a house or home. A **dweller** is a person who lives in a certain place.

elevated raised up or lifted up onto a high level. **Elevation** is the height of a certain area.

enlarge to grow or increase in size

fatigue tiredness. If you are **fatigued**, you are very weary, tired, or exhausted.

federal having to do with or belonging to the U.S. government

formation a structure or an arrangement; the act of building or developing

frequency the condition of occurring often

heeded to have listened and followed advice or a warning

inquire to ask about something in order to get information

interval the distance or space between two things; the period of time between two events

moderate mild; not large, great, or severe

plight a serious or dangerous situation

portions sections of a larger whole

refresh to refill or replenish; to make almost new

rely to depend on somebody or something; to have confidence in

restore to repair; to bring something back to its original condition. If something has been **restored**, it has been repaired or put back in place. **Restoration** is the act of repairing something.

secure safe; free from danger

somber sad or serious

technique a method or procedure

tiring exhausting; becoming in need of rest

topple to push or fall over

turmoil excitement or confusion

undergo to experience something. Someone who has **undergone** a change has experienced something new or different.

version a description or retelling that usually gives one point of view

vicinity the area surrounding a place

withstand to oppose, resist, or survive. Something that has been **withstood** has been opposed or resisted.

Index